The accompaniment CD included with this book
has pipe organ accompaniments for 40 carols and
and is coordinated with all editions of

Christmas Carols
for Friends and Families
with "Where do our carols come from?"

The accompaniment CD included with this book has pipe organ accompaniments for 40 of the 84 carols and rounds in *Christmas Carols for Friends and Families*. Now you can enjoy singing carols even though you may not have a "live" accompanist! The order of carols on the CD matches the order in the book, as does the number of stanzas played. The playing is "straight" - no free accompaniments or varied harmonizations - which permits you to sing in parts, and to add instrumentalists to your singing. An instrument (piano or other) can play along, even with a free "descant" of the performer's creating if desired, because the performer will know exactly what the organ is going to play.

The most familiar carols are in order, as found in the front of the book: sacred #1 through #18, secular #19 through 27 (omitting 25). Some "requests" follow. To sing any particular carol, go directly to its track on the CD. If you wish to sing fewer than all stanzas, you can push "STOP" after the number of stanzas you wish to sing. (The organ plays all stanzas, so you are always able to sing all stanzas if you wish.) With someone working the CD player, you can select which carols to sing in what order, as well as how many stanzas to include. To learn the rounds, sing them with the CD, and then try singing them without the CD, in two, three, or four parts.

Joan Welles sings "O holy night" on this CD, as she sings it for us at our carol parties. That, and "Upon this holy night" can be presented as solos, or you can "sing along" with her.

Refer to the Index on the back cover to find the track numbers of the recorded carols.

edited by Adrienne Tindall
DARCEY PRESS - Box 5018, Vernon Hills, IL 60061
www.darceypress.com

First printing June, 1995
Second printing May, 1996
Third printing December, 1997
Fourth printing September, 1998
Fifth printing September, 1999
Sixth printing September, 2000
Seventh Printing August, 2001
Eighth Printing (with CD) August, 2002

ISBN 1-889079-37-5

1. O come, all ye faithful

(Adeste, fideles)

1. O come, all ye faith - ful, joy - ful and tri - um - phant, O come ye, O
2. Sing choirs of an - gels, sing in ex - ul - ta - tion, ____ Sing, all ye
3. *A - des - te, fi - de - les, lae - ti tri - um - phan - tes; ve - ni - te, ve -*

come ____ ye to Beth - le - hem. Come and be - hold him,
cit - i - zens of heav'n ____ a - bove: Glo - ry to God ____
ni - te in Beth - le - hem. Na - tum vi - de - te

born the king of an - gels: O come let us a - dore him, O come, let us a -
in the high-est, glo - ry! O come let us a - dore him, O come, let us a -
Re - gem an - ge - lor - um. Ve - ni - te a - do - re - mus, ve - ni - te a - do -

dore him, O come let us a - dore him, ____ Christ ____ the Lord.
dore him, O come let us a - dore him, ____ Christ ____ the Lord.
re - mus, ve - ni - te a - do - re - mus, ____ Do - - mi - num.

Text: Latin Hymn; attr. John F. Wade, ca. 1743; translation, Frederick Oakeley, 1841, and others; alt.
Tune: ADESTE FIDELES: John F. Wade's *Cantus Diversi*, 1751

2. The first nowell

1. The first no-well, the an-gel did say was to cer-tain poor shep-herds in
2. They look-ed up and saw a star shin-ing in the East be-
3. This star drew nigh to the north-west, o'er Beth-le-hem it
4. Then en-tered in there Wise-men three, full rev-'rent-ly up-

fields as they lay; in fields where they lay keep-ing their sheep on a
yond them far, and to the earth it gave great light, and
took its rest, and there it did both stop and stay right
on their knee, and of-fer'd there, in his pres-ence, their

cold win-ter's night that was so deep.
so it con-tin-ued both day and night. *Chorus*
o-ver the place where Je-sus lay. No - well, no - well, no-
gold and myrrh and frank - in-cense.

well, no - well, born is the King of Is - ra - el.

Text: Traditional English carol, 17th C.
Tune: THE FIRST NOWELL: W. Sandys' *Christmas Carols*, 1833; arranged John Stainer, 1871

3. It came upon the midnight clear

1. It came up-on the mid-night clear, that glor-ious song of old, from
2. Still through the clo-ven skies they come, with peace-ful wings un-furled; and
3. For lo! the days are has-tening on, by proph-ets seen of old, when

an - gels bend - ing near the earth, to touch their harps of gold: "Peace
still their heav'n - ly mus - ic floats o'er all the wea - ry world. A -
with the ev - er - cir - cling years shall come the time fore - told, when

on the earth, good-will to men from heav'n's all gra - cious King!" The
bove its sad and low - ly plains they bend on hov - 'ring wing, and
the new heav'n and earth shall own the Prince of Peace their King, and

world in sol - emn still - ness lay to hear the an - gels sing.
ev - er o'er its Ba - bel sounds the bless - ed an - gels sing.
the whole world send back the song which now the an - gels sing.

Text: Edmund Hamilton Sears, 1849
Tune: CAROL: Richard Storrs Willis, 1850

4. While shepherds watched their flocks

1. While shepherds watched their flocks by night, all seated on the ground, the angel of the Lord came down, and glory shone around, and glory shone around.

2. "Fear not," said he, for mighty dread had seized their troubled minds. "Glad tidings of great joy I bring to you and all mankind, to you and all mankind.

3. "To you in David's town this day is born of David's line the Savior, who is Christ the Lord, and this shall be the sign, and this shall be the sign:

4. The heav'nly Babe you there shall find to human view displayed, all meanly wrapped in swathing bands, and in a manger laid, and in a manger laid."

5. Thus spake the seraph, and forthwith appeared a shining throng of angels, praising God, who thus addressed their joyful song, addressed their joyful song:

6. "All glory be to God on high, and to the earth be peace; good will henceforth from heav'n to earth begin and never cease, begin and never cease!"

Text: Nahum Tate,. 1700, alt.
Tune: CHRISTMAS: *Harmonia Sacra*, 1812; arranged from G. F. Handel, 1728

5. Hark! the herald angels sing

1. Hark! the her - ald an - gels sing, __ "Glo - ry to the new - born King!
2. Christ, by high - est heav'n a - dored; __ Christ, the ev - er - last - ing Lord!
3. Hail the heav'n - born Prince of Peace! __ Hail the Sun of Right-eous-ness!

Peace on earth and mer - cy mild, __ God and sin - ners rec - on - ciled."
Late in time be - hold him come, __ off - spring of the fa - vored one.
Light and life to all he brings, _ ris'n with heal - ing in his wings.

Joy - ful, all ye na - tions, rise, __ join the tri - umph of the skies; __
Veiled in flesh, the God - head see; __ hail th'in - car - nate De - i - ty!
Mild he lays his glo - ry by, __ born that man no more may die, __

with th'an - gel - ic hosts pro - claim, "Christ is __ born in Beth - le - hem."
Pleased, as man with men to dwell, Je - sus, __ our Em - man - u - el!
born to raise the sons of earth, born to __ give them sec - ond birth.

Hark! the her - ald an - gels sing, "Glo - ry __ to the new - born King!"

Text: Charles Wesley, 1739; alt. by George Whitefield, 1753, and others
Tune: MENDELSSOHN: Felix Mendelssohn, 1840, adapted by William H. Cummings, 1855

6. Angels, from the realms of glory

1. An - gels, from the realms of glo - ry, wing your flight o'er
2. Shep - herds, in the fields a - bid - ing, watch - ing o'er your
3. Sa - ges, leave your con - tem - pla - tions; bright - er vi - sions
4. Saints, be - fore your al - tar bend - ing, watch - ing long in

all the earth; ye who sang cre - a - tion's sto - ry,
flocks by night, God with man is now re - sid - ing,
beam a - far; seek the great De - sire of na - tions,
hope and fear, sud - den - ly the Lord, de - scend - ing,

Refrain

now pro - claim Mes - si - ah's birth: come and wor - ship,
yon - der shines the ___ in - fant Light:
ye have seen his ___ na - tal star:
in his tem - ple ___ shall ap - pear:

come and wor - ship, wor - ship Christ, the new - born King.

Text: James Montgomery, 1816, 1825, alt.
Tune: REGENT SQUARE: Henry T. Smart, 1867

7. Angels we have heard on high

1. An - gels we have heard on high, sweet - ly sing - ing o'er the plains,
2. Shep - herds, why this ju - bi - lee? Why your joy - ous songs pro - long?
3. Come to Beth - le - hem and see him whose birth the an - gels sing;

and the moun - tains, in re - ply, ech - o - ing their joy - ous strains.
What the glad - some tid - ings be which in - spire your heav'n - ly song?
come, a - dore on bend - ed knee Christ the Lord, the new - born King.

Refrain

Glo - - - - - - - - - ri - a

in ex - cel - sis De - o, Glo - - - - - - -

- - - - ri - a in ex - cel - sis De - - o.

Text: Traditional French carol, 18th C.; translation *Crown of Jesus Music,* 1862, alt.
Tune: GLORIA: Traditional French melody; arranged by Edward Shippen Barnes, 1937

8. Good Christians all, rejoice
(In dulci jubilo)

1. Good Christ-ians all, re - joice_____ with heart and soul and voice;_____
2. Good Christ-ians all, re - joice_____ with heart and soul and voice;_____
3. Good Christ-ians all, re - joice_____ with heart and soul and voice;_____
4. *In dul - ci ju - bi - lo_____ Nun sing - et und seid froh!_____*

Give ye heed to what we say: Je - sus Christ is born to - day;
now ye hear of end - less bliss: Je - sus Christ is born for this!
now ye need not fear the grave: Je - sus Christ was born to save!
Un - sers Herz - ens Won - ne leit in prae-sep - i - o,_____ und

ox and ass be - fore him bow, and he is in the man - ger now.
He hath o - pened heav - en's door, and we are blest for - ev - er - more.
Calls you one and calls you all to gain his ev - er - last - ing hall.
leuch - tet als die Son - ne ma - tris in grem - i - o._____

Christ is born to - day!_____ Christ is born to - day!_____
Christ was born for this!_____ Christ was born for this!_____
Christ was born to save!_____ Christ was born to save!_____
Al - pha es et O!_____ Al - pha es et O!_____

Text: Medieval macaronic carol; translated and paraphrased, John Mason Neale, 1853, alt.
Tune: IN DULCI JUBILO: German folk tune 14th C.; harmonization AT, 1995

9. God rest you merry, gentlemen

1. God rest you merry, gentlemen, let no-thing you dis-may; re-
2. From God our heaven-ly Fa - ther a bless-ed an - gel came, and
3. "Fear not," then said the an - gel, "let noth-ing you af - fright; this
4. Now to the Lord sing prais - es, all you with-in this place, and

mem - ber Christ our Sav - ior was born on Christ-mas day to
un - to cer-tain shep - herds brought ti - dings of the same, how
day is born a Sav - ior of a pure vir - gin bright, to
with true love and bro - ther-hood each oth - er now em - brace; this

save us all from Sa - tan's power when we were gone a - stray.
that in Beth - le - hem was born the Son of God by name.
free all those who trust in him from Sa - tan's power and might."
ho - ly tide of Christ - mas all oth - ers doth re - place.

Refrain

O ___ ti - dings of com - - - fort and joy, com-fort and

joy; O ___ ti - dings of com - fort and joy.

Text: English carol, 18th C., alt.
Tune: GOD REST YOU MERRY: Traditional melody, harmonization AT, 1995

10. O little town of Bethlehem

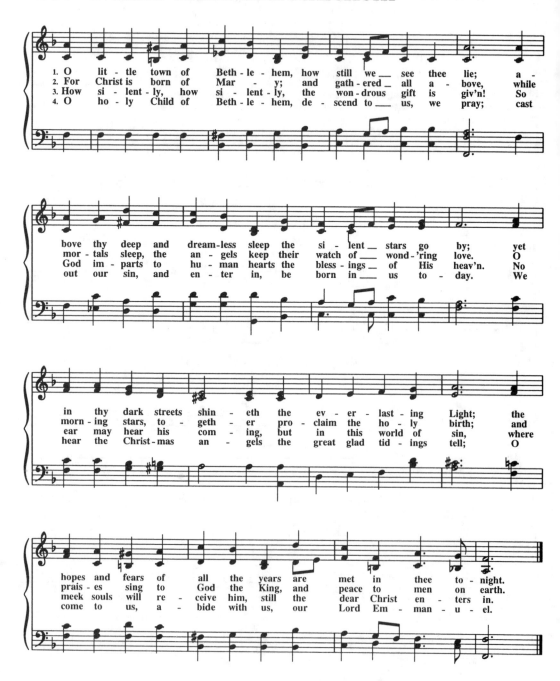

1. O little town of Beth - le - hem, how still we __ see thee lie; a -
2. For Christ is born of Mar - y; and gath - ered __ all a - bove, while
3. How si - lent - ly, how si - lent - ly, the won - drous gift is giv'n! So
4. O ho - ly Child of Beth - le - hem, de - scend to __ us, we pray; cast

bove thy deep and dream-less sleep the si - lent __ stars go by; yet
mor - tals sleep, the an - gels keep their watch of __ wond - 'ring love. O
God im - parts to hu - man hearts the bless - ings __ of His heav'n. No
out our sin, and en - ter in, be born in __ us to - day. We

in thy dark streets shin — eth the ev - er - last - ing Light; the
morn - ing stars, to - geth — er pro - claim the ho - ly birth; and
ear may hear his com — ing, but in this world of sin, where
hear the Christ - mas an - gels the great glad tid - ings tell; O

hopes and fears of all the years are met in thee to - night.
prais - es sing to God the King, and peace to men on earth.
meek souls will re - ceive him, still the dear Christ en - ters in.
come to us, a - bide with us, our Lord Em - man - u - el.

Text: Phillips Brooks, 1868
Tune: ST. LOUIS: Lewis H. Redner, 1868

And it came to pass in those days, that there went out a decree from Cæsar Augustus, that all the world should be taxed. ... And all went to be taxed, every one into his own city. And Joseph also went up from Galilee, out of the city of Nazareth, into Judæa, unto the city of David, which is called Bethlehem; (because he was of the house and lineage of David:) to be taxed with Mary his espoused wife, being great with child. And so it was, that, while they were there, the days were accomplished that she should be delivered. And she brought forth her firstborn son, and wrapped him in swaddling clothes, and laid him in a manger; because there was no room for them in the inn.

And there were in the same country shepherds abiding in the field, keeping watch over their flock by night. And, lo, the angel of the Lord came upon them, and the glory of the Lord shone round about them: and they were sore afraid. And the angel said unto them, Fear not: for, behold, I bring you good tidings of great joy, which shall be to all people. For unto you is born this day in the city of David a Saviour, which is Christ the Lord. And this shall be a sign unto you; ye shall find the babe wrapped in swaddling clothes, lying in a manger. And suddenly there was with the angel a multitude of the heavenly host praising God, and saying, Glory to God in the highest, and on earth peace, good will toward men.

And it came to pass, as the angels were gone away from them into heaven, the shepherds said one to another, Let us now go even unto Bethlehem, and see this thing which is come to pass, which the Lord hath made known unto us. And they came with haste, and found Mary, and Joseph, and the babe lying in a manger. And when they had seen it, they made known abroad the saying which was told them concerning this child. And all they that heard it wondered at those things which were told them by the shepherds. ... And the shepherds returned, glorifying and praising God.   Luke 2: 1-20

11. Child in the manger

1. Child in the man - ger, in - fant of Mar - y,
2. This the most ho - ly Child of sal - va - tion
3. Pro - phets fore - told him, in - fant of won - der;

out - cast and strang - er, Lord _ of all! Child who in - her - its
gent - ly and low - ly lived _ be - low; he is the glo - rious
an - gels be - hold him on _ his throne; worth - y our Sav - ior

all our trans-gres - sions, all our de - mer - its on _ him fall.
might - y Re - deem - er, see him vic - tor - ious o - ver each foe.
of all their prais - es; hap - py for - ev - er are _ his own.

Text: *Leanabh an aigh*, Gaelic song by Mary Macdonald of Mull, 19th C.; translation Lachlan Macbean, 1888, alt.
NOTE: This is the original association of text to BUNESSAN.
Tune: BUNESSAN: Hebridean melody from the Isle of Mull; harmonization AT, 1995

12. Away in a manger

1. A - way in a_ man-ger, no_ crib for a bed, the_ lit - tle Lord
2. The cat - tle are_ low-ing, the_ Ba - by a - wakes, but_ lit - tle Lord

Je - sus laid_ down his sweet head. The stars in the_ hea - vens looked
Je - sus, no_ cry - ing he makes. I love thee, Lord_ Je - sus, look_

down where he lay, the_ lit - tle Lord Je - sus, a - sleep on the hay.
down from the sky, and_ stay by my side un - til_ morn - ing is nigh.

Text: as found in *Little Children's Book for Schools and Families*, ca. 1885
Tune: CRADLE SONG: William James Kirkpatrick, 1895; harmonization AT, 1995

13. Away in a manger

1. A - way in a man-ger, no crib for his bed, the lit - tle Lord Je - sus laid down his sweet head. The
2. The-cat - tle are low-ing, the Ba - by a - wakes, but lit - tle Lord Je - sus, no cry - ing he makes. I

stars in the heav-ens looked down where he lay, the lit - tle Lord Je - sus, a - sleep on the hay.
love thee, Lord Je - sus, look down from the sky, and stay by my side un - til morn - ing is nigh.

Text: as found in *Little Children's Book for Schools and Families*, ca. 1885
Tune: MUELLER: attributed to James R. Murray, 1887

14. What child is this?

1. What child is this _ who, laid to rest, _ on Mar - y's lap _ is sleep - ing? Whom
2. So bring him in - cense, gold, and myrrh, come peas - ant, king _ to own him; the

an - gels greet _ with an - thems sweet, _ while shep - herds watch _ are keep - ing?
King of kings _ sal - va - tion brings; _ let lov - ing hearts _ en - throne him.

This, this _ is Christ the King, _ whom shep - herds guard, _ and an - gels sing:
Raise, raise _ the song on high; _ the Vir - gin sings _ her lull - a - by:

haste, haste _ to bring him laud, _ the Babe, _ the Son _ of Mar - y.
joy, joy, _ for Christ is born, _ the Babe, _ the Son _ of Mar - y.

Text: William Chatterton Dix, ca. 1865
Tune: GREENSLEEVES: ca. 16th C. English melody

15. Silent night, holy night!
(Stille Nacht, heilige Nacht!)

1. Si - lent night, ho - ly night! All is calm, all is bright
2. Si - lent night, ho - ly night! Shep - herds quake - at the sight!
3. Si - lent night, ho - ly night! Son of God, Love's pure light
4. *Stil - le Nacht, hei - li - ge Nacht! Al - les schläft, ein - sam wacht*

'round yon vir - gin mo - ther and child! Ho - ly in - fant, so ten - der and mild,
Glo - ries stream from heav - en a - far, heav'n-ly hosts sing Al - le - lu - ia,
ra - diant beams from thy ho - ly face, with the dawn of re - deem - ing grace,
nur das trau - te hoch - hei - li - ge Paar, Hol - der Kna - be mit lok - ki - gen Haar,

sleep in heav - en - ly peace! Sleep in heav - en - ly peace.
Christ, the Sav - ior, is born! Christ, the Sav - ior, is born!
Je - sus, Lord, at thy birth, Je - sus, Lord, at thy birth.
schlaf in himm - li - scher Ruh, schlaf in himm - li - scher Ruh.

Text: Joseph Mohr, 1818; translation John Freeman Young, 1863
Tune: STILLE NACHT: Franz Xaver Gruber, 1818

Now when Jesus was born in Bethlehem of Judæa in the days of Herod the king, behold, there came wise men from the east to Jerusalem, saying, Where is he that is born King of the Jews? for we have seen his star in the east, and are come to worship him. When Herod the king had heard these things, he was troubled, and all Jerusalem with him. And when he had gathered all the chief priests and scribes of the people together, he demanded of them where Christ should be born. And they said unto him, In Bethlehem of Judæa: for thus it is written by the prophet, And thou Bethlehem, in the land of Juda, art not the least among the princes of Juda: for out of thee shall come a Governor, that shall rule my people Israel.

Then Herod, when he had privily called the wise men, inquired of them diligently what time the star appeared. And he sent them to Bethlehem, and said, Go and search diligently for the young child; and when ye have found him, bring me word again, that I may come and worship him also. When they had heard the king, they departed; and, lo, the star, which they saw in the east, went before them, till it came and stood over where the young child was.

When they saw the star, they rejoiced with exceeding great joy. And when they were come into the house, they saw the young child with Mary his mother, and fell down, and worshipped him: and when they had opened their treasures, they presented unto him gifts; gold, and frankincense, and myrrh.

Matthew 2:1-11

16. We three kings of Orient are

1. We three kings of O - ri - ent are, bear - ing gifts we
2. Born a babe on Beth - le - hem's plain, gold I bring to
3. Frank - in - cense to of - fer have I; In - cense owns a
4. Myrrh is mine; its bit - ter per - fume breathes a life of
5. Glo - rious now be - hold him a - rise, King and God and

tra - verse a - far field and foun - tain, moor and moun - tain,
crown him a - gain, King for - ev - er, ceas - ing nev - er,
De - i - ty nigh, pray'r and prais - ing all men rais - ing,
gath - er - ing gloom; sor - rowing, sigh - ing, bleed - ing, dy - ing,
Sac - ri - fice; heav'n sings, "Hal - le - lu - jah!" "Hal - le -

Chorus

fol - low - ing yon - der star.
o - ver us all to reign.
wor - ship God on high. Oh, _____ star of won - der,
sealed in the stone - cold tomb.
lu - jah!" earth re - plies.

star of might, star with roy - al beau - ty bright, west - ward

lead - ing, still pro - ceed - ing, guide us to the per - fect light.

Text: John Henry Hopkins, Jr., 1857
Tune: THREE KINGS OF ORIENT: John Henry Hopkins, Jr., 1857

17. Fairest Lord Jesus

1. Fair - est Lord Je - - sus, ru - ler of all
2. Fair are the mead - - ows, fair - er still the
3. Fair is the sun - - shine, fair - er still the

na - ture, O thou of God and ___ man the
wood - lands, robed in the bloom - ing ___ garb of
moon - light, and all the twin - kling, ___ star - ry

Son, thee will I cher - ish, thee will I
spring: Je - sus is fair - er, Je - sus is
host: Je - sus shines bright - er, Je - sus shines

hon - or, thou, my soul's glo - ry, joy, and crown!
pur - er, who makes the woe - ful heart to sing.
pur - er, than all the an - gels heaven can boast.

Text: *Gesangbuch*, Münster, 1677; translation anonymous, 1850
Tune: CRUSADER'S HYMN: J. Hoffman von Fallersleben's *Schlesische Volkslieder*, 1842; arranged Richard Storrs Willis, 1850

18. Joy to the world!

1. Joy to the world! The Lord is come; let earth re-
2. Joy to the world! The Savior reigns; let men their
3. No more let sin and sorrow grow, nor thorns in-
4. He rules the world with truth and grace, and makes the

ceive her King; let ev-'ry heart prepare him
songs employ; while fields and floods, rocks, hills and
fest the ground; he comes to make his bless-ings
na-tions prove the glo-ries of his right-eous-

room, and heav'n and na-ture sing, and heav'n and na-ture
plains, re-peat the sound-ing joy, re-peat the sound-ing
flow, far as the curse is found, far as the curse is
ness, and won-ders of his love, and won-ders of his

(1) and heav'n and na-ture sing,

(1) and

sing, and heav'n, and heav'n and na-ture sing.
joy, re-peat, re-peat the sound-ing joy.
found, far as, far as the curse is found.
love, and won-ders, and won ders of his love.

heav'n and na-ture sing,

Text: Isaac Watts, 1719
Tune: ANTIOCH: from G. F. Handel, 1742; arranged by Lowell Mason, 1848

19. Deck the halls

1. Deck the halls with boughs of hol - ly, fa la la la la la la la la.
2. See the blaz - ing Yule be - fore us, fa la la la la la la la la.
3. Fast a - way the old year pass - es, fa la la la la la la la la.

'Tis the sea - son to be jol - ly, fa la la la la la la la la.
Strike the harp and join the cho - rus, fa la la la la la la la la.
Hail the new, ye lads and lass - es, fa la la la la la la la la.

Don we now our gay ap - par - el, fa la la la la la la la,
Fol - low me in mer - ry meas - ure, fa la la la la la la la,
Sing we joy - ous all to - geth - er, fa la la la la la la la,

troll the an - cient Yule - tide car - ol, fa la la la la la la la la.
while I tell of Yule - tide treas - ure, fa la la la la la la la la.
heed - less of the wind and weath - er, fa la la la la la la la la.

Text: Traditional Welsh
Tune: NOS GALAN: Traditional Welsh air

20. Here we come a wassailing

1. Here we come a - was - sail-ing, a - mong the leaves so green,_____
2. God bless the mas - ter of this house, and bless the mis - tress, too,_____ and

here we come a - wan - d'ring, so fair____ to be seen; love and
all the lit - tle chil - dren that 'round the ta - ble go;

joy come to you, and to you your was - sail too, and God

bless you, and send____ you a hap - - py new

year, and God send you a hap - py new year.

Text: Traditional North of England
Tune: WASSAIL SONG: Traditional North of England; harmonization AT, 1995

21. Jingle bells!

1. Dash - ing thro' the snow in a one - horse o - pen sleigh, and
2. Day or two a - go I thought I'd take a ride,
3. Now the ground is white, go it while you're young;

o'er the fields we go, laugh - ing all the way; The
soon Miss Fan - nie Bright was seat - ed by my side. The
take the girls to - night, and sing this sleigh-ing song; The just

bells on bob - tail ring, mak - ing spir - its bright; what
horse was lean and lank, mis - for - tune seemed his lot, he
get a bob - tailed nag, two for - ty for his speed, then

fun it is to ride and sing a sleigh - ing song to - night! Oh,
got in - to a drift - ed bank, and we, we got up - sot. Oh,
hitch him to an o - pen sleigh, and crack! you'll take the lead. Oh,

Refrain

jin - gle bells! Jin - gle bells! Jin - gle all the way!

Text: James Pierpont, 1857
Tune: James Pierpont, 1857, harmonization AT 1995

Oh, what fun it is to ride in a one horse o-pen sleigh! ____

Jin - gle bells! Jin - gle bells! Jin - gle all the way!

Oh, what fun it is to ride in a one horse o - pen sleigh! ____

22. Jingle, jingle, jingle (4-part round)

1. Jin - gle, jin - gle, jin - gle, jin - gle, jin - gle bells!

2. Jin - gle, jin - gle, jin - gle bells!

3. Jin - gle, jin - gle, jin - gle, jin - gle, jin - gle bells!

4. Jin - gle, jin - gle, jin - gle bells!

Round: Adrienne Tindall, 1995

23. Jolly old Saint Nicholas

1. Jol - ly old Saint Ni - cho - las, lean your ear this way!
2. When the clock is strik - ing twelve, when I'm fast a - sleep,
3. John - ny wants a pair of skates, Su - sy wants a dol - ly;

Don't you tell a sin - gle soul what I'm going to say;
down the chim - ney broad and black, with your pack you'll creep;
Nel - lie wants a sto - ry book; she thinks dolls are fol - ly;

Christ-mas Eve is com - ing soon; now, you dear old man,
all the stock - ings you will find hang - ing in a row;
as for me, my lit - tle brain is - n't ver - y bright;

whis - per what you'll bring to me; tell me if you can.
mine will be the short - est one, you'll be sure to know.
choose for me, old San - ta Claus, what you think is right.

Text: Anonymous, traditional
Tune: Traditional

24. O Christmas tree
(O Tannenbaum)

1. O Christ-mas tree, O Christ-mas tree, how faith-ful is your col-or! O Christ-mas tree, O Christ-mas tree, how faith-ful is your col-or! So fresh and green in sum-mer's breeze, still deep-ly green through win-ter's freeze. O Christ-mas tree, O Christ-mas tree, how faith-ful is your col-or!

2. O Christ-mas tree, O Christ-mas tree, how love-ly is your beau-ty! O Christ-mas tree, O Christ-mas tree, how love-ly is your beau-ty! And oft-en is my Christ-mas-time blest by the fra-grance of a pine. O Christ-mas tree, O Christ-mas tree, how love-ly is your beau-ty!

3. O Christ-mas tree, O Christ-mas tree, your stead-fast green can teach me: O Christ-mas tree, O Christ-mas tree, your stead-fast green can teach me of strength and hope, fi-del-i-ty, of com-fort and sta-bil-i-ty. O Christ-mas tree, O Christ-mas tree, your stead-fast green can teach me!

4. O Tan-nen-baum, O Tan-nen-baum, wie treu sind dei-ne Blät-ter! O Tan-nen-baum, O Tan-nen-baum, wie treu sind dei-ne Blät-ter! Du grünst nicht nur zur Som-mers-zeit, nein, auch im Win-ter, wenn es schneit. O Tan-nen-baum, O Tan-nen-baum, wie treu sind dei-ne Blät-ter!

Text: Ernst Anschütz, ca. 1824; translation AT, 1995
Tune: O TANNENBAUM: German carol, ca. 1800; harmonization AT, 1995

25. The twelve days of Christmas

Text: Traditional English, ca. 19th C.
Tune: Traditional English: arrangement AT, 1995

two tur-tle-doves, and a par-tridge in a pear tree. 6.-12. On the

repeat for each number, counting down

sixth day of Christ-mas my true love sent to me six geese a - lay-ing,
sev-enth day of Christ-mas my true love sent to me seven swans a - swim-ming,
eighth day of Christ-mas my true love sent to me eight maids a - milk-ing,
ninth day of Christ-mas my true love sent to me nine la - dies danc-ing,
tenth day of Christ-mas my true love sent to me ten lords a - leap-ing,
'lev-enth day of Christ-mas my true love sent to me 'leven pi - pers pip-ing,
twelfth day of Christ-mas my true love sent to me twelve drum-mers drum-ming,

five gold __ rings, four __ call-ing birds, three French hens,

two __ tur-tle-doves, and a par-tridge in a pear tree.

26. Up on the house-top

1. Up on the house-top __ rein-deer pause, out jumps good old San - ta Claus;
2. First comes the stock-ing of lit - tle Nell; oh, dear San - ta, fill it well;
3. Next comes the stock-ing of lit - tle Will; oh, just see what a glor - ious fill!

down through the chim-ney with lots of toys, all for the lit - tle ones' Christ-mas joys.
give her a dol - ly that laughs and cries, one that will o - pen and shut her eyes.
Here is a ham - mer and lots of tacks, al - so a ball __ and a whip that cracks.

Chorus

Ho, ho, ho! Who would-n't go? Ho, ho, ho! Who would-n't go? __

Up on the house-top, click, click, click! Down through the chim-ney with good Saint Nick.

Text: Benjamin Russell Hanby, mid 19th C.
Tune: Benjamin Russell Hanby, mid 19th C.

27. We wish you a merry Christmas

We wish you a merry Christmas, we wish you a merry Christmas, we wish you a merry Christmas, and a happy New Year! Good ti - dings we bring to all of you here; good ti - dings for Christ - mas and a hap - py New Year! We

Fine

Text: Traditional English folksong
Tune: Traditional English carol; harmonization AT, 1995

28. A baby sleeps within a stall

(Ein Kindlein in der Wiegen)

1. A baby sleeps within a stall, a tiny little one; _____ his face is shining, mirroring light as warm as an holy sun, _____ this tiny little one. _____

2. The babe, so humbly cradled there is Jesus Christ, the Lord. He gives his peace, inspires with his love! Fulfilling God's holy Word is Jesus Christ, our Lord.

3. And all who feel the love of Christ will have his blessèd care; will keep, within, a heart that is pure, just like his mother fair, with purity everywhere. _____

4. *Ein Kindlein in der Wiegen, ein kleines Kindelein, _____ das gleisst gleich wie ein Spiegel nach Adelichem Schein, _____ das kleine Kindelein. _____*

Text: Austrian, 1649, as found in *Geistliche Nachtigal*, 1649; translation AT, 1995
Tune: EIN KINDLEIN IN DER WIEGEN: *Geistliche Nachtigal*, 1649; harmonization AT, 1995

29. *A la nanita nana*

Text: Traditional Spanish; translation AT, 1995
Tune: Traditional Spanish carol; harmonization AT, 1995

30. All my heart this night rejoices

1. All my heart this night re-joic - es, as I
2. Hark, a voice from yon - der man - ger; soft and
3. Come, then, let us has - ten yon - der; here let

hear, far and near, sweet - est an - gel voi - - ces:
sweet doth en - treat, "Flee from woe and dan - - ger;
all, great and small, kneel in awe and won - der.

"Christ is born," their choirs are sing - ing, till the
peo - ple come: from all that grieves you, till you are
Love him who with love is yearn - ing; hail the

air ev - ery - where now with joy is ring - ing.
freed; all you need I will sure - ly give you."
star that from far bright with hope is burn - ing!

Text: Paul Gerhardt, 1653; translation Catherine Winkworth, 1858, alt.
Tune: WARUM SOLLT' ICH: Johann Georg Ebeling, 1666

31. As with gladness men of old

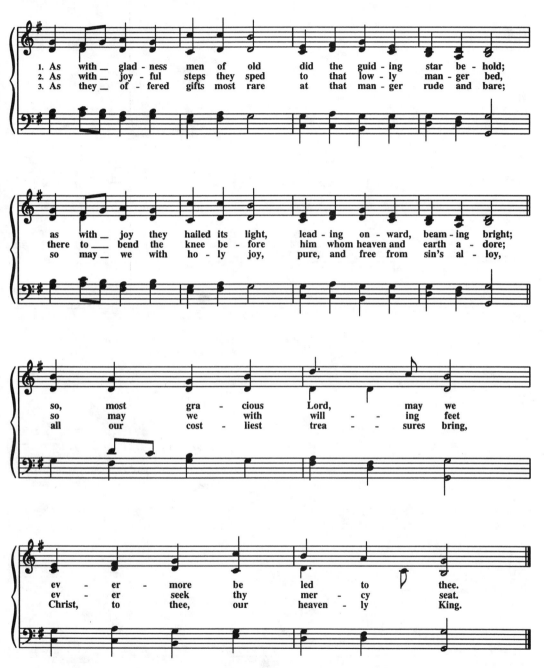

1. As with gladness men of old did the guiding star behold;
as with joy they hailed its light, leading onward, beaming bright;
so, most gracious Lord, may we evermore be led to thee.

2. As with joyful steps they sped to that lowly manger bed,
there to bend the knee before him whom heaven and earth adore;
so may we with willing feet ever seek thy mercy seat.

3. As they offered gifts most rare at that manger rude and bare;
so may we with holy joy, pure, and free from sin's alloy,
all our costliest treasures bring, Christ, to thee, our heavenly King.

Text: William Chatterton Dix, 1860
Tune: DIX: adapted by William Henry Monk, 1861, from a chorale by Conrad Kocher, 1838

32. Break forth, O beauteous heavenly light
(Brich an, du schönes Morgenlicht)

1. Break forth, O beau-teous heav'n-ly light, and ush-er in the morn - ing; O shep-herds, shrink _ not with af - fright, but hear the an - gel's warn - ing. This child, now weak in in - fan-cy, our con - fi - dence and joy shall be, the power of Sa - tan break - ing, our peace e - ter - nal mak - ing.

2. *Brich an, du schö-nes Mor-gen-licht, und lass den Him-mel ta - gen; du Hir-ten-volk _ er-stau - ne nicht, weil dir die En - gel sa - gen, dass die - ses schwa - che Knä - be-lein soll un - ser Trost _ und Freu - de sein, da - zu dein Sa - tan zwin - gen, und al - les wie-der _ bring - en.*

Text: Johann Rist, 1641; translation John Troutbeck, ca. 1885
Tune: ERMUNTRE DICH: Johann Schop, 1641; harmonization J. S. Bach, 1734

33. Bring your torches, Jeannette, Isabella

(Un flambeau, Jeannette, Isabelle)

1. Bring your tor - ches, Jean - nette, Is - a - bel - la, bring your
2. Hush your voi - ces, the ba - by is sleep - ing; hush your
3. Soft - ly, come to the child in the man - ger, soft - ly,

tor - ches, make haste and come! Ma - ry calls us to
voi - ces, your talk - ing should cease. Though you're shar - ing your
come to this ho - ly place. Wel - come Je - sus, our

Beth - le - hem's man - ger; Je - sus is born! Let all a -
joy at his com - ing, chat - ter - ing words dis - turb his
beau - ti - ful Sav - ior; he is so fair, his cheeks so

dore him! Ah, ah, beau - ti - ful is the moth - er!
slum - ber. Ah, ah, qui - et - ly he is rest - ing,
ros - y! Ah, ah, see how he smiles while sleep - ing;

Ah, ah, beau - ti - ful is the son!
ah, ah, see how he sleeps in peace.
ah, ah, beau - ti - ful is his face.

Text: Traditional Provençal, *Cantiques de Primiére Advenement de Jèsus-Christ*, 1553; translation AT, 1995
Tune: Provençal Carol, *Cantiques de Primiére Advenement de Jèsus-Christ*, 1553; harmonization AT, 1995

34. Ding dong! Merrily on high

1. Ding dong! Mer-ri - ly on high in heav'n the bells are ring - ing:
2. E'en so here be - low, be - low, let stee - ple bells be swung - en,
3. Pray you, du - ti - ful - ly prime your mat - in chime, ye ring - ers;

Ding ding! Ver-i - ly the sky is riv'n with an - gel sing - ing.
And, i - o, i - o, i - o, by priest and peo - ple sung - en.
may you beau-ti - ful - ly rime your eve - time song, ye sing - ers.

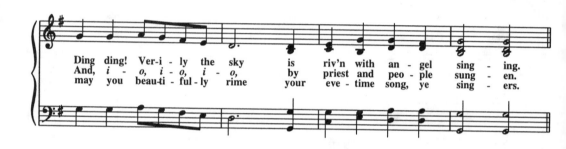

Refrain

Glo —

- - - - - ri - a, ho - san - na in ex - cel - sis!

Text: George R. Woodward, ca. 1900
Tune: 16th century French melody, harmonization AT, 1995

35. From a far-off land
(De tierra lejana venimos)

1. From a far-off land we've tra-veled here to greet him, guid-ed by the star, which led our steps to meet him.
2. To the new-born Babe, a King of kings most ten-der, I have brought pure gold, to touch his life with splen-dor.
3. To the Son of God my frank-in-cense is giv-en; fra-grance filled with soul, whose beau-ty reach-es heav-en.
4. To the heaven-ly Child, who comes to bring earth glad-ness, I have brought this myrrh, to com-fort him in sad-ness.

Refrain

See the shin-ing star, which her-alds earth's new dawn-ing! May its heal-ing ra - diance shine and nev-er cease! ___ Glor-y in the heights to Christ, our ho-ly Sav - ior! Glor-y in the heights! And on the earth be love and joy and peace. ___

Text: Traditional Puerto Rican, translation AT, 1995
Tune: Traditional Puerto Rican, harmonization AT, 1995

36. From heaven above to earth I come

(Vom Himmel hoch)

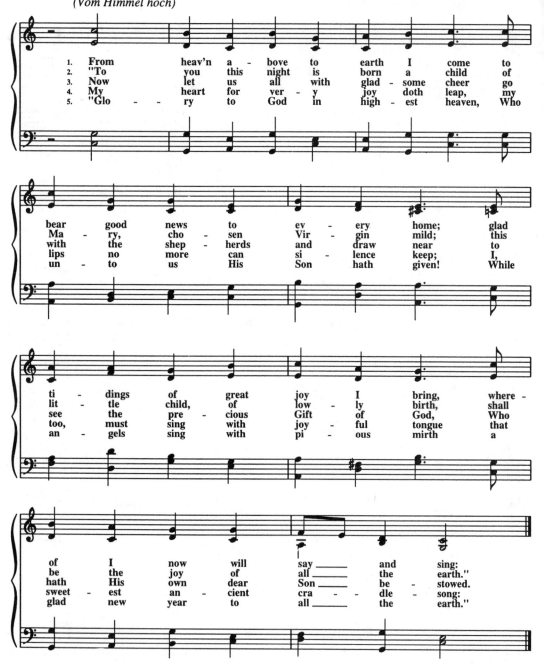

1. From heav'n a - bove to earth I come to
2. "To you this night is born a child of
3. Now let us all with glad - some cheer go
4. My heart for ver - y joy doth leap, my
5. "Glo - ry to God in high - est heaven, Who

bear good news to ev - ery home; glad
Ma - ry, cho - sen Vir - gin mild; this
with the shep - herds and draw near to
lips no more can si - lence keep; I,
un - to us His Son hath given! While

ti - dings of great joy I bring, where -
lit - tle child, of low - ly birth, shall
see the pre - cious Gift of God, Who
too, must sing with joy - ful tongue that
an - gels sing with pi - ous mirth a

of I now will say ____ and sing:
be the joy of all ____ the earth."
hath His own dear Son ____ be - stowed.
sweet - est an - cient cra - - dle - song:"
glad new year to all ____ the earth."

Text: Martin Luther, 1535; translation Catherine Winkworth, 1855, alt.
Tune: VOM HIMMEL HOCH: Schumann's *Geistliche Lieder,* 1539

37. *Fum, fum, fum!*

1. On De-cem-ber five and twen-ty, *fum, fum, fum!* On De-cem-ber
2. Lit-tle birds from leaf-y wood-lands, *fum, fum, fum!* Lit-tle birds from
3. Lit-tle stars up in the heav-ens, *fum, fum, fum!* Lit-tle stars up

five and twen-ty, *fum, fum, fum!* he was born, the ho-ly
leaf-y wood-lands, *fum, fum, fum!* leave your nest-lings home to
in the heav-ens, *fum, fum, fum!* you may see the ba-by

Child, for love of us, the Un-de-filed. It was cold the night his
sing, and fly to see the new-born King. Build a nest of warmth and
cry, but let no tear-drops dim your eye, for the dark of night is

Moth-er, Mar-y, bore our eld-er bro-ther. *Fum, fum, fum!*
shar-ing, that the Babe will feel your car-ing. *Fum, fum, fum!*
end-ing in the clear, pure light you're send-ing. *Fum, fum, fum!*

Text: Traditional Catalonian carol; translation AT, 1995
Tune: Traditional Catalonian carol; harmonization AT, 1995

38. Gentle Mary laid her child

1. Gen-tle Mar-y laid her child low-ly in a man-ger;
2. An-gels sang a-bout his birth; wise men sought and found him;
3. Gen-tle Mar-y laid her child low-ly in a man-ger;

there he lay, the un-de-filed, to the world a strang-er.
heav-en's star shone bright-ly forth, glo-ry all a-round him.
he is still the un-de-filed, but no more a strang-er.

Such a babe in such a place; can he be the Sav-ior?
Shep-herds saw the won-drous sight, heard the an-gels sing-ing;
Son of God, of hum-ble birth, beau-ti-ful the sto-ry;

Ask the saved of all the race who have found his fa - - vor.
all the plains were lit that night, all the hills were ring - - ing.
praise his name in all the earth, hail the King of Glo - - ry!

Text: Joseph Simpson Cook, 1919
20Tune: TEMPUS ADEST FLORIDUM: *Piae Cantiones*, 1582; harmonization AT, 1995

39. Go tell it on the mountain

Go, tell it on the moun - tain, o - ver the hills and ev - ery - where;
go tell it on the moun - tain that Je - sus Christ is born.

1. While shep - herds kept their watch - ing o'er si - lent flocks by night, be -
2. The shep - herds feared and trem - bled when, lo! a - bove the earth rang
3. Down in a low - ly man - ger the hum - ble Christ was born, and

hold, through - out the heav - ens there shone a ho - ly light. ___
out the an - gel cho - rus that hailed our Sav - ior's birth. ___
God sent us sal - va - tion that bless - ed Christ - mas morn. ___

Text: John W. Work, 1907
Tune: GO TELL IT: Afro-American Spritual, harmonization AT, 1995

40. He is born, the holy One!
(Il est né, le divin Enfant)

Refrain

He is born, the ___ ho - ly One! Play the ___ o - boes, ___ sound the trum - pets! He is born, the ___ ho - ly One! Shout with joy that ___ he is come! *Fine*

1. For four thou - sand ___ years and more,
2. Ah, his ___ grace brings ___ health and joy,
3. In a sta - ble he finds a home,
4. Je - sus, King from ___ heaven a - bove,

Text: French carol, 19th C.; translation AT, 1995
Tune: IL EST NÉ: traditional French melody, 18th C.; harmonization AT, 1995

pro - phets vowed that ____ he was com - ing;
beau - ty of a ____ pure per - fec - tion!
finds his bed in a straw - filled man - ger,
yet a ti - ny ____ babe be - fore us,

for four thou - sand ____ years and more
Ah, his grace brings ____ health and joy;
in a sta - ble he finds a home,
Je - sus, King from ____ heaven a - bove,

D.C.

we've a - - wait - ed this Ad - vent hour.
gen - tle, pure, this ____ ho - ly boy!
Son of God, how ____ hum - bly come!
rule our hearts with ____ your pure love!

D.C.

41. How brightly beams the morning star!
(Wie schön leuchtet der Morgenstern)

1. How bright-ly beams the morn-ing star! What sud - den ra - diance from a - far doth
2. *Wie schön leuch-tet der Mor-gen-stern, voll Gnad' und Wahr-heit von dem Herrn, die*

glad us with its shin - ing? Bright-ness of God, that breaks our night and
süss-e Wur-zel Jes - se! Du Sohn Da-vids aus Ja - kobs Stamm, mein

fills the dark-ened souls with light who long for truth were pin - ing!
Kö - nig und mein Bräu-ti-gam, hast mir mein Herz be - sess - en.

Thy word, Je - sus, in-ly feeds us, right-ly leads us,
Lieb - lich, freund-lich, schön und herr-lich, gross und ehr-lich,

life be-stow - ing. Praise, O praise such love o'er-flow - ing!
Reich und Ga - ben, hoch und sehr präch-tig er-hab - en.

Text: Philipp Nicolai, 1598; translation Catherine Winkworth, 1863
Tune: WIE SCHÖN LEUCHTET DER MORGENSTERN: Philipp Nicolai, 1598; harmonization J. S. Bach, ca. 1731

42. I heard the bells on Christmas day

1. I heard the bells on Christmas day their old familiar carols play, and
2. I thought how, as the day had come, the belfries of all Christendom had
3. And in despair I bowed my head. "There is no peace on earth," I said, "for
4. Then pealed the bells more loud and deep. "God is not dead, nor doth He sleep; the
5. Till, ringing, singing on its way, the world revolved from night to day; a

wild and sweet the words repeat of peace on earth, good will to men.
rolled along th'unbroken song of peace on earth, good will to men.
hate is strong, and mocks the song of peace on earth, good will to men."
wrong shall fail, the right prevail, with peace on earth, good will to men."
voice, a chime, a chant sublime, of peace on earth, good will to men!

Text: Henry Wadsworth Longfellow, 1863
Tune: WALTHAM: Jean Baptiste Calkin, 1872

43. I saw three ships

1. I saw three ships come sailing in on Christmas day, on Christmas day; I
2. And what was in those ships all three, on Christmas day, on Christmas day; and
3. The Virgin Mary and Christ were there, on Christmas day, on Christmas day; the

saw three ships come sailing in on Christmas day in the morning.
what was in those ships all three, on Christmas day in the morning?
Virgin Mary and Christ were there, on Christmas day in the morning.

4. Pray, whither sailed those ships all three?
5. O, they sailed into Bethlehem.
6. And all the bells on earth shall ring,

7. And all the angels in heaven shall sing,
8. And all the souls on earth shall sing.
9. Then let us all rejoice amain!

Text: Traditional English
Tune: Traditional English, harmonization Sir John Stainer, ca. 1875

44. In the bleak midwinter

1. In the bleak mid-winter, frost-y wind made moan,
earth stood hard as i - ron, wa-ter like a stone;
snow had fal-len, snow on snow, snow on snow,
in the bleak mid-win-ter, long a-go.

2. An-gels and arch-an-gels may have gath-ered there,
cher-u-bim and ser-a-phim throng-éd the air;
but his moth-er on-ly, in her maid-en bliss,
wor-shiped the be-lov-ed with a kiss.

3. What can I give him, poor as I am?
If I were a shep-herd, I would bring a lamb;
if I were a Wise Man, I would do my part;
what I can I give him: give my heart.

Text: Christina G. Rossetti, 1872
Tune: CRANHAM: Gustav Holst, 1906

45. Infant holy
(W zlobie lezy)

1. In - fant ho - ly, in - fant low - ly, for his bed a cat - tle stall; ox - en
2. Flocks were sleep - ing, shep-herds keep - ing vig - il till the morn-ing new saw the

low - ing, lit - tle know - ing Christ the babe is Lord of all. Swift are
glo - ry, heard the sto - ry, tid - ings of a gos - pel true. Thus re -

wing - ing an - gels sing - ing, no - els ring - ing, tid - ings bring - ing: Christ the
joic - ing, free from sor - row, prais-es voic - ing, greet the mor - row: Christ the

babe is Lord of all; Christ the babe is Lord of all.
babe was born for you; Christ the babe was born for you.

Text: Traditional Polish Carol, translated and paraphrased Edith M. G. Reed, 1925
Tune: W ZLOBIE LEZY: traditional Polish melody: harmonization AT, 1995

46. It could be Bethlehem

1. It could be Bethlehem, upon ___ a hill, with
2. And there could be to-night, as there ___ was then, a
3. It could have been that star that shines ___ a-bove which
4. And there could be in us a ho - ly birth of

1. qui - et shep - herds watch - ing o - ver sheep, ___ for
2. mul - ti - tude ___ of an - gels sing - ing praise ___ to
3. shone up - on ___ the man - ger babe that night. ___ And
4. Christ - li - ness ___ here in this pres - ent place ___ to

1. in this cit - y now ___ we list - en still, ___ and
2. God, and pro - mis - ing ___ sweet peace to men, ___ if
3. it could lead as sure - ly to his love, ___ if
4. bring a - gain up - on ___ this trou - bled earth ___ the

1. in ___ our ways a Christ - - - mas vig - il keep.
2. we ___ would seek the Christ ___ in all our ways.
3. we ___ let rays of truth ___ make our lives bright.
4. glad ___ na - tiv - i - ty ___ of truth and grace.

Text: Max Dunaway, alt. Words from the *Christian Science Sentinel.* © 1970 The Christian Science Publishing Society. Used with permission.
Tune: DUNAWAY: Adrienne Tindall, 1980

Tune and Arrangement based on the solo arrangement Copyright © 1986 Adrienne Tindall.
Used with permission.

47. Jesus, our brother, kind and good
(The friendly beasts)

1. Je-sus, our broth-er, ___ kind and good, was ___ hum-bly born in a
2. "I", said the cow, all ___ white and red, "I gave him my man-ger ___
3. "I", said the dove from the raf-ters high, "I cooed him to sleep that he

sta-ble rude, and the friend-ly beasts a-round ___ him stood;
for his bed, I ___ gave him my hay to pil-low his head.
should not cry, we ___ cooed him to sleep, my mate ___ and I,

Je-sus, our broth-er, kind ___ and good. "I," said the don-key, shag-gy and
I", said the cow, ___ all white and red. "I," said the sheep with cur-ly
I," said the dove from the raft-ers high. Thus ev-'ry beast by some ___ good

brown, "I ___ car-ried his moth-er ___ up-hill and down; I ___ car-ried his
horn, "I ___ gave him my wool for his blan-ket warm, he ___ wore my
spell, in the sta-ble dark was ___ glad ___ to tell how he gave ___ his

moth-er to Beth-le-hem town. ___ I," said the don-key shag-gy and brown.
coat ___ on Christ-mas morn. ___ I," said the sheep with cur-ly horn.
gift to Em-man-u-el; the gift ___ he gave Em-man-u-el.

Text: French carol, 12th C.; translation anonymous
Tune: ORIENTIS PARTIBUS: early 13th C., harmonization AT, 1995

48. Joseph *lieber*, Joseph mine

(Song of the crib)

(Mary) 1. Jo — seph *lie* — — *ber*, Jo — — seph mine,
(Joseph) 2. Glad — ly, *lie* — — *be*, love — — ly one,
(1st Servant) 3. Christ — ians, now re — joice — and sing!
(2nd servant) 4. God's own ev — er — last — — ing Word,

help me rock the child di — vine!
I will rock your lit — — tle son,
Sure — — ly does this heaven — — ly King
ev — — er — pres — — ent, vir — — tuous Lord,

God's re — ward — ing will be thine in heav — en, for the
God's re — ward — ing will be done in heav — en for the
free us from ev — ery sin — ful thing: of pur — est birth, the
pre — cious Truth, by all a — dored in heaven and earth, the

Chorus

Son of Vir — — gin Mar — — y.
Son of Vir — — gin Mar — — y.
Son of Vir — — gin Mar — — y.
Son of Vir — — gin Mar — — y.   He

Text: Traditional German, 15th C.; translation AT, 1995
Tune: RESONET IN LAUDIBUS: Traditional German, 15th C.; harmonization AT, 1995

comes to us this ve - ry day, this ve - ry day in

Is - ra - el. Mar - y heard the news pro - claimed by

Ga - bri - el. Ei - a, ei - a,

Je - sus Christ is born to us of Mar - y.

49. Joyful singing (4 part round)

List - en to the an - gel song; see the heav - ens filled with light;

join your voi - ces, sing a - long: peace to all the earth this night.

Round: Adrienne Tindall, 1995

50. Let all mortal flesh keep silence

1. Let all mor-tal flesh keep __ si - lence, and with fear and
2. King of kings, yet born of __ Ma - ry, as of old on
3. Rank on rank the host of __ heav - en spreads its van - guard

trem - bling __ stand; pon - der noth-ing earth - ly __ mind - ed,
earth he __ stood, Lord of lords, in hu - man __ ves - ture,
on the __ way, as the Light of light de - scend - eth

for with bless - ing in his __ hand Christ the Lord to earth de -
in the bod - y and the __ blood, he will give to all the
from the realms of end - less __ day, that the powers of hell may

scend - - eth, our full hom - age to de - mand.
faith - - ful, his own self for heaven - ly food.
van - - ish as the dark - ness clears a - way.

Text: *Liturgy of St. James*, 4th C., adapt. Gerard Moultrie, 1864
Tune: PICARDY: Traditional French melody, 17th C.; harmonization *English Hymnal*, 1906

51. Lo, how a Rose e'er blooming

(Es ist ein Ros' entsprungen)

1. Lo, how a Rose e'er bloom-ing from ten-der stem hath sprung!
2. I - sa - iah 'twas fore-told it, the Rose I have in mind,
3. This Flow'r whose fra-grance ten - der with sweet-ness fills the air,
4. Es ist ein Ros' ent-sprung-en aus ein - er Wur - zel zart,

Of Jes-se's lin-eage com - ing as seers of old have sung.
with Ma - ry we be-hold it, the vir - gin mo - ther kind.
dis - pels with glor-ious splen-dor the dark-ness ev - ery-where.
wie uns die Al - ten sung - en, aus Jes - se kam die Art;

It came a flow'r-et bright, _____ a - mid the
To show God's love a-right _____ she bore to
True man, the Son of God, _____ from sin and
und hat ein Blüm - lein bracht, _____ mit - ten im

cold of win - ter, when half - spent was the night.
us a Sa - vior, when half - spent was the night.
death he saves us and light - ens ev - 'ry load.
kal - ten Win - ter, wohl zu der hal - ben Nacht.

Text: German 15th C., translation Theodore Baker, 1894, alt.
Tune: ES IST EIN ROS': *Alte Catholische Geistliche Kirchengesäng*, 1599; arranged Michael Praetorius, 1609

52. Love came down at Christmas

1. Love came down at Christ-mas, love all love-ly, love _ di - vine;
2. Wor - ship we _ the God - head, love in - car - nate, love _ di - vine;
3. Love shall be _ our to - ken, love be yours _ and love _ be mine;

love was born _ at Christ-mas; — star and an - gels gave _ the sign.
wor - ship we _ our Je - sus — what shall be _ our sa - cred sign?
love to God _ and neigh - bor, love for prayer and gift _ and sign.

Text: Christina Rossetti, 1883, alt.
Tune: AMOR: © Austin C. Lovelace, 1995. Used with permission of the composer.

53. Lullay, thou little tiny child
(Coventry carol)

1. Lul - lay, thou lit - tle ti - ny Child, by, by, lul - ly, lul - lay; _____ lul -
2. O sis - ters too, how may we do, for to pre - serve this day _____ this
3. Her - od, the king, in his rag - ing charg-ed he hath this day _____ his
4. Then woe is me, poor Child, for thee, and ev - er mourn and say; _____ for

lay, thou lit - tle ti - ny Child, by, by, lul - ly, lul - lay. _____
poor Young-ling for whom we sing by, by, lul - ly, lul - lay? _____
men of might, in his own sight, all chil-dren young, to slay. _____
thy part - ing nor say nor sing by, by, lul - ly, lul - lay. _____

Text: Robert Croo, 1534
Tune: Ancient English melody, 15th C.

54. Maria walked 'mid thornwood trees

(Maria durch den Dornwald ging)

1. Ma - ri - a walked 'mid thorn - wood ___ trees,
2. Ma - ri - a car - ried un - der her heart,
3. The trees bore leaves and flowers at ___ last,

Ky - ri - e e - le - i - son. Ma - ri - a walked 'mid ___
Kr - ri - e e - le - i - son, Ma - ri - a car - ried ___
Ky - ri - e e - le - i - son. The ___ trees bore leaves and ___

thorn - wood trees: for ___ sev - en years they had
un - der her heart the ___ ho - ly babe who would
flowers at last, as Ma - ri - a and her ___

borne no leaves: Je - sus and Ma - ri - a.
life im - part: Je - sus and Ma - ri - a.
babe went past: Je - sus and Ma - ri - a.

Text: Traditional German, ca. 1500; translation AT, 1995
Tune: German medieval carol, ca. 1500; harmonization AT, 1995

55. Noels! New noels!

(Noel nouvelet)

1. No - els! New no - els! ___ Let us ___ sing no -
el! Let God hear the mes - sage
that our ___ car - ols tell: thanks be to God for
earth's new ___ King. No - els! New no -
els! ___ Let all ___ peo - ple sing!

2. An - gels told the shep - herds: leave your ___ flocks of
sheep. Seek th'an - gel - ic ba - - by
where he's ___ fast a - sleep. Find your soul's rest and
find your heart's joy. No - els, New no -
els! ___ to the ___ ba - by boy.

3. Shep - herds came to - geth - er; Beth - lehem ___ was the
place; Jo - seph knelt with Ma - - ry,
by the ___ child of grace cra - dled in safe - ty
in a ___ stall. No - els! New no -
els! ___ Now sing ___ one and all.

Text: Traditional French carol, translation AT, 1995
Tune: NOEL NOUVELET: traditional French, harmonization AT, 1995

56. O come, little children

1. O come, lit - tle chil - dren, O come, one and all, to
2. He's born in a sta - ble for you and for me, draw
3. See Mar - y and Jo - seph with love - beam - ing eyes are
4. Kneel down and a - dore him with shep - herds to - day, lift

Beth - le - hem haste, to the man - ger so small. God's
near - by the bright gleam - ing star - light to see, in
gaz - ing up - on the rude bed where he lies, in the
up lit - tle hands now, and praise him as they; re -

Son for a gift has been sent you this night, to
swad - dling clothes ly - ing, so meek and so mild, and
shep - herds are kneel - ing, with hearts full of love, while
joice that a Sav - ior from sin you can boast, and

be your Re - deem - er, your Joy and De - light.
pur - er than an - gels, the heav - en - ly Child.
an - gels sing loud al - le - lu - ias a - bove.
join in the song of the heav - en - ly host.

Text: Christoph von Schmid, ca. 1800; translator unknown
Tune: IHR KINDERLEIN KOMMET: Johann Schulz, ca. 1780

57. O come, O come, Emmanuel

1. O come, O come, Em-man-u-el, and ran-som cap-tive
2. O come, thou Day-spring, come and cheer our spir-its by thine
3. O come, De-sire of na-tions, bind all peo-ples in one

Is-ra-el that mourns in lone-ly ex-ile here un-
ad-vent here; dis-perse the gloom-y clouds of night, and
heart and mind; bid thou our sad di-vis-ions cease, and

Refrain

til the Son of God ap-pear.
death's dark shad-ows put to flight. Re-joice! Re-joice! Em-
be thy-self our King of Peace.

man-u-el shall come to thee, O Is-ra-el.

Text: Medieval Latin antiphons; translations composite
Tune: VENI EMMANUEL: 15th C. melody, adapted; harmonization AT, 1995

58. O holy night
(Cantique de Noël)

1. O ho - ly night, ____ the stars are bright-ly
2. Tru - ly he taught us to love ____ one an-
3. *Mi - nuit, Chrè-tien, ____ c'est l'heu - re so - len-*

shin - ing, it is the night of the dear Sav-ior's birth;
oth - er; his law is love and his gos - pel is peace.
nel - le où l'Homme-Dieu des - cen-dit jus - q'uà nous,

long lay the
Chains shall he
pour ef - fa-

world __ in sin and er - ror pin - ing, till he ap-peared and the soul felt its
break, for the slave is our broth - er, and in his name all op-pres - sion shall
cer __ la tache o - ri - gi - nel - le et de son père ar - rê - ter le cour-

worth. A thrill of hope the wea-ry soul re - joic - es, for yon - der breaks a
cease. Sweet hymns of joy in grate-ful cho-rus raise we, let all with - in us
roux. Le mon - de en - tier tres - sail - le d'es-pé - ran - ce a cet - te nuit qui

Text: Cappeau de Roquemaure; translation John S. Dwight, 19th C.
Tune: CANTIQUE DE NOEL, Adolphe Adam, 19th C.

59. O how happy! O how holy!
(O sanctissima!)

1. O how hap - py! __ O how ho - ly! __
2. O how hap - py! __ O how ho - ly! __
3. O how hap - py! __ O how ho - ly! __
4. O sanc - tis - si - ma, O pi - - is - si - ma __

1. Christ - mas comes with its grace and joy!
2. Christ - mas comes with its grace and joy!
3. Christ - mas comes with its grace and joy!
4. dul - cis Vir - go Ma - ri - - - a,

1. Love re - deems a world for - lorn; Christ the Sa - vior now is born!
2. Christ will fill the world with light, end - ing shad - ows of our night!
3. Heaven - ly hosts re - joice to sing glo - ry to our Sav - ior King!
4. ma - ter a - ma - ta, in - te - me - ra - ta,

1. Praise __ him, __ praise __ this ho - ly boy!
2. Praise __ him, __ praise __ this ho - ly boy!
3. Praise __ him, __ praise __ this ho - ly boy!
4. o - - ra, __ o - - ra pro no - - - bis.

Text: from the Latin: German translation, Johannes Falk, 1816; English translation of the German, AT, 1995
Tune: SICILIAN HYMN: 18th C. Italian; harmonization AT, 1995

60. O Jesu sweet
(O Jesulein Süss)

1. O Jesu sweet, O Jesu mild, the Son of God, the bless - ed Child! You came to earth from heav'n a - bove; your hu - man life re - deems through love, O Je - su sweet, O Je - su mild.

2. O Jesu sweet, O Jesu mild, your love re - stores us un - de - filed! Our debts ac - know - ledged, and for - given through God's own grace you bring from heaven, O Je - su sweet, O Je - su mild.

3. O Jesu sweet, O Jesu mild, in Love's re - flect - ing, heav - en has smiled! Ig - nite in us Love's per - fect flame: O make us worth - y of your name, O Je - su sweet, O Je - su mild!

4. O Je - su - lein süss, O Je - su - lein mild, des Va - ters Will - en hast du er - füllt. Bist kom - men aus dem Him - mel - reich, uns ar - men Mensch - en wor - den gleich, O Je - su - lein süss, O Je - su - lein mild.

Text: Samuel Scheidt, 1650, translation AT, 1995
Tune: O JESULEIN SÜSS: Samuel Scheidt, 1650, harmonization J. S. Bach

61. Of the Father's love begotten

1. Of the Fa - ther's love be - got - ten, ere the worlds be - gan to be,
2. O ye heights of heaven a - dore him; an - gel hosts, his prais - es sing;

he is Al - pha and O - me - ga, he the source, the end - ing he;
powers, do - min - ions, bow be - fore him, and ex - tol our God and King;

of the things that are, that have been,
let no tongue on earth be si - lent,

and that fu - ture years shall see, ev - er - more and ev - er - more!
ev - ery voice in con - cert ring, ev - er - more and ev - er - more!

Text: Aurelius Clemens Prudentius, 4th C.; st. 1 translation John Mason Neale, 1854, alt.; st. 2 Henry W. Baker, 1859
Tune: DIVINUM MYSTERIUM: 13th C. Plainsong, Mode V: harmonization AT, 1995

62. On Christmas night all Christians sing

(Sussex carol)

1. On Christ - mas night all Christ - ians sing, to
2. Then why should men on earth ___ be sad, since
3. When sin de - parts be - fore ___ his grace, then
4. All out of dark - ness we ___ have light, which

hear the news ___ the an - gels bring, on Christ-mas night all Christ - ians sing to
our Re - deem - er makes us glad, then why should men on earth ___ be sad, since
life and health . come in its place; when sin de - parts be - fore ___ his grace, then
made the an - gels sing this night: all out of dark - ness we ___ have light, which

hear the news ___ the an - gels bring; news of great joy, ___ news of ___ great
our Re - deem - er makes us glad; when from our sin ___ he set ___ us
life and health _ come in its place; an - gels and men ___ with joy ___ may
made the an - gels sing this night; "Glo - ry to God ___ and peace _ to

mirth, news of our mer - ci - ful ___ King's birth.
free, all for to gain our lib - er - ty?
sing, all for to see the new - born King.
men, now and for - ev - er-more. ___ A - men."

Text: Traditional English
Tune: SUSSEX CAROL, traditional melody, harmonization AT, 1995

63. On this day earth shall ring

1. On this day earth shall ring with the song
2. His the doom, ours the mirth when he came
3. God's bright star o'er his head, wise men three
4. On this day an - gels sing, with their song

chil - dren sing to the Lord Christ our King, born on earth to save us,
down to earth, Beth-le - hem saw his birth; ox and ass be - side him
to him led; kneel-ing low by his bed, lay their gifts be - fore him,
earth shall ring, prais-ing Christ, heav - en's King, born on earth to save us,

him the Fa - ther gave us: *I - de - o - o - o, i - de - o -
from the cold would hide him:
praise him and a - dore him:
peace and love he gave us:

o - o, i - de - o glo - ri - a in ex - cel - sis De - o!

* "Ideo"(ee-day-oh) is "therefore" in Latin

Text: *Piae Cantiones* 1582; translation Jane M. Joseph, 1924
Tune: PERSONENT HODIE: *Piae Cantiones* 1582; arranged by Gustav Holst, 1925, alt.

64. Once in royal David's city

1. Once in roy - al Da - vid's _ cit - y stood a low - ly cat - tle _ shed, where a moth - er laid _ her _ ba - by - in a man - ger for _ his _ bed; Ma - ry, lov - - ing moth - er mild, _ Je - sus Christ her lit - tle _ child. _

2. He came down to earth _ from _ heav - en, he who is the Lord _ of _ all, and his shel - ter was _ a _ sta - ble, and his cra - dle was _ a _ stall. With the poor, the scorned, the low - ly lived on earth the Sav - ior _ ho - ly.

3. And our eyes at last _ shall _ see him, through his own re - deem - ing _ love; for that child so dear _ and _ gen - tle is our Lord in heav'n . a - bove; and he leads his chil - dren on _ to the place where he _ is _ gone.

Text: Cecil Frances Alexander, 1848, alt.
Tune: IRBY: Henry J. Gauntlett, 1849, harmonization Arthur Henry Mann, 1919, alt.

65. Rise up, shepherd, and follow

1. There's a star in the east on __ Christ-mas morn, rise up, shep-herd, and fol-low; it - 'll
2. If you take good. heed to the an - gels' words, rise up shep-herd, and fol-low; you'll for -

lead to the place where the Sav-ior's born, __ rise up, shep-herd, and fol-low.
get your _ flocks, you'll for - get your herds, __ rise up, shep-herd, and fol-low.

Leave your ewes and leave your lambs, rise up shep-herd, and fol-low.

Leave your sheep and leave your rams, rise up shep-herd, and fol-low.

Fol - low, fol - low, rise up, shep-herd, and fol-low.

Fol - low the star of Beth le - hem, __ rise up shep-herd, and fol-low.

Text: African-American spiritual, 19th C.
Tune: RISE UP, SHEPHERD: African-American spiritual, 19th C.; harmonization AT, 1995

66. Rock-a-bye, my dear little boy

(Rocking Carol)

1. Rock-a - bye, my dear lit - tle boy, dear lit - tle boy, won - der of won - ders, my
2. Lit - tle Je - sus, In - fant Di - vine, In - fant Di - vine, one with the Fa - ther, yet

bless - ing and joy; slum - ber as I gent - ly hold you,
born to be mine; as I rock you calm - ly sleep - ing,

let my ten - der love en - fold you; gift of God to
an - gel guards their watch are keep - ing; pre - cious child, one

me and the world, here in my arms lies so peace - ful - ly curled.
day we shall see what love has des - tined for you and for me.

Text: Czech carol, Translation by Jaroslav J. Vajda. Copyright © 1987, Concordia Publishing House. Used with permission.
Tune: ROCKING: Czech carol; harmonization AT, 1995

67. Shepherds! Shake off your drowsy sleep

1. Shep - herds! Shake off your drow - sy sleep, rise and leave your sil - ly sheep; an - gels from heav'n a - round loud sing - ing, ti - dings of great joy are bring - ing.

2. Hark! E - ven now the bells ring 'round; lis - ten to their mer - ry sound; hark! How the birds new songs are mak - ing, as if win - ter's chains were break - ing. Shep-herds! the

3. See how the flow'rs all burst a - new, think - ing snow is sum - mer dew; see how the stars a - fresh are glow - ing, all their bright - est beams be - stow - ing.

cho - rus come and swell! Sing No - ël, O sing No - ël!

Text: Traditional French Carol; translation anonymous
Tune: BESANÇON CAROL: Traditional French

68. Sing with the Angels

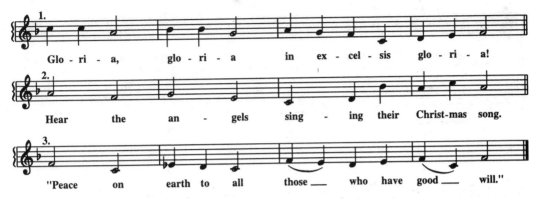

Glo - ri - a, glo - ri - a in ex - cel - sis glo - ri - a!

Hear the an - gels sing - ing their Christ-mas song.

"Peace on earth to all those __ who have good __ will."

69. Still, still, still

1. "Still, __ still, __ still; sleep still, my __ babe, sleep __ still!" The
2. "Sleep, __ sleep, __ sleep; my ba - by, __ rest in __ sleep. God's
3. *Still, __ still, __ still, weil's Kind-lein __ schla-fen __ will.* *Ma -*

Moth-er a qui - et watch is keep-ing; close on her breast the Sav - ior is sleep-ing.
an - gels will sing their ex - ul - ta - tion; greet-ing your birth with sweet jub-i - la - tion;
ri - a __ tut es nie - der sing-en, ih - re __ keu - sche Brust zu __ bring-en,

"Still, __ still, __ still; sleep still, my babe, sleep still."
sleep, __ sleep, __ sleep; my ba - by, rest in sleep."
still, __ still, __ still, weil's Kind - lein schla-fen __ will.

Text: Traditional Austrian, translation AT, 1995
Tune: Salzburg melody, 1819; harmonization AT, 1995

70. That boy-child of Mary

Refrain (unison)

That boy-child of Ma—ry was born in a sta—ble, a man-ger his cra—dle in Beth-le-hem.

Fine

1. What shall we call him, child of the man—ger? What name is giv—en in Beth-le-hem?
2. His name is Je—sus, God ev-er with us, God giv-en for us in Beth-le-hem.
3. How can he save us, how can he help us, born here a-mong us in Beth-le-hem?
4. Gift of the Fa—ther, to hu-man moth-er, makes him our broth-er of Beth-le-hem.
5. One with the Fa—ther, he is our Sav-ior, heav-en-sent help-er of Beth-le-hem.
6. Glad-ly we praise him, love and a-dore him, give our-selves to him of Beth-le-hem.

D.C.

Text: Tom Colvin, 1969
Tune: BLANTYRE: Traditional Malawi melody, adapted by Tom Colvin, 1969

71. The holly and the ivy

1. The hol - ly and the i - vy, when they are both full
2. The hol - ly bears a blos - som, as white as li - ly
3. The hol - ly bears a ber - ry, as red as an - y
4. The hol - ly bears a prick - le, as sharp as an - y
5. The hol - ly bears a bark, as bit - ter as an - y

grown, of all the trees that are in the wood, the
flow'r, and Ma - ry bore sweet Je - sus Christ to
blood, and Ma - ry bore sweet Je - sus Christ to
thorn, and Ma - ry bore sweet Je - sus Christ on
gall, and Ma - ry bore sweet Je - sus Christ for

hol - ly bears the crown:
be our sweet Sa - vior:
do poor sin - ners good: the ris - ing of the
Christ - mas day in the morn:
to re - deem us all:

sun and the run - ning of the deer, the play - ing of the

mer - ry or - gan, sweet sing - ing in the choir.

Text: Traditional English carol, ca. 1700
Tune: Traditional English melody, harmonization AT, 1995

72. The snow lay on the ground
(Venite adoremus)

1. The snow lay on the ground, ___ the star shone bright, ___ when
2. 'Twas Ma - ry, Vir - gin pure, ___ of ho - ly Anne, ___ that
3. Saint Jo - seph, too, was by ___ to tend the Child; ___ to

Christ our Lord was born on Christ - mas night. ___ Ve -
brought in - to this world the God - made man. ___ She
guard him and pro - tect his mo - ther mild; ___ the

ni - te a - do - re - mus Do - mi - num, ___ ve -
laid him in a stall at Beth - le - hem, ___ the
an - gels hov - ered 'round, and sang this song: ___ ve -

Text: Traditional English carol, ca. 1860
Tune: VENITE ADOREMUS: English melody, adapted C. Winfred Douglas; harmonization AT, 1995

ni - te a - do - re - mus Do - mi - num. _____ Ve -
ass and ox - en shared the roof with them. _____ Ve -
ni - te a - do - re - mus Do - mi - num. _____

ni - te a - do - re - mus Do - mi - num, _____ ve -

ni - te a - do - re - mus Do - mi - num. _____

73. There's a song in the air

Text: Josiah G. Holland, 1874
Tune: CHRISTMAS SONG: Karl P. Harrington, 1904

74. To us in Bethlem city

1. To us in Beth - lem cit - y was born a lit - tle
2. And all our love and for - tune lie in his might - y
3. O Shep - herd, ev - er near us, we'll go where thou dost
4. No grief shall part us from thee, how - ev - er sharp the

Son; in him all gen - tle gra - - ces were
hands; our sor - rows, joys, and fail - - ures he
lead; no mat - ter where the pas - - ture, with
edge; we'll serve and do thy bid - - ding O

gath - ered in - to one: O joy:
sees and un - der - stands: O joy:
thee at hand to feed: O joy:
take our hearts in pledge! O joy:

glad joy! were gath - ered in - to one.
glad joy! he sees and un - der - stands.
glad joy! with thee at hand to feed.
glad joy! O take our hearts in pledge.

Text: Percy Dearmer; based on a carol in *Cölner Psalter*, 1638
Tune: BETHLEM CITY: Melody in *Cölner Psalter*, 1638

75. 'Twas in the moon of wintertime

1. 'Twas in the moon of win-ter-time, when all the birds had
2. With-in a lodge of bro-ken bark the ten-der Babe was
3. O chil-dren of the for-est free, O you of Man-i

fled, that might-y Gitch-i Man-i-tou** sent
found; a rag-ged robe of rab-bit skin en-
tou, the Ho-ly Child of earth and heaven is

an-gel choirs in-stead. Be-fore their light the
wrapped his beau-ty 'round. The chiefs from far be-
born to-day for you. Come kneel be-fore the

**Almighty God

Text: Native American (Huron): Jean de Brébeuf, c. 1641: translation J. E. Middleton, 1926
English Text used by permission of The Frederick Harris Company. All rights reserved.
Tune: UNE JEUNE PUCELLE, French Carol, 16th century, harmonization AT, 1995

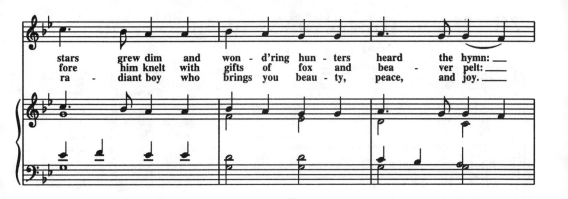

stars grew dim and won - d'ring hun - ters heard the hymn: __
fore him knelt with gifts of fox and bea - ver pelt: __
ra - diant boy who brings you beau - ty, peace, and joy. __

"Je - sus, your King is born; Je - sus is

born! *In ex - cel - sis glo - ri - a!"* __

Stanza 1 in Huron

Esteiaron de tsonoue,
Jesous ahatonhia.
Onna-ouate oua d'oki n'ou
ouanda skoua en tak.
En nonchien skouatchi hotak,
n'on ouandi lonra chata,
Jesous ahatonhia,
Jesous ahatonhia, Jesous ahatonhia.

76. Upon this blessèd night

(El Cant dels Ocells)

1. Up - on this bless - ed night there shines a heaven - ly
2. As rul - ers of the air, whose worlds touch ev - ery -
3. Their mes - sage ech - oes clear: "Our Christ - mas - time is
4. O may my heart take wing, and fly to greet my

light that reach - es ev - ery na - tion. The
where, they send their car - ols wing - ing: "The
here! The an - gels tell the sto - ry. Let
King, whom Ma - ry shields from dan - ger. Be -

birds be - gin to sing; they cel - e - brate a King who
Sav - ior comes to earth; come cel - e - brate his birth! O
all the earth re - joice! Let grat - i - tude find voice, and
hold, this God - sent boy, who brings us peace and joy, is

Text: Translation AT, 1995: based on and inspired by *"El Cant dels Ocells"*, traditional Catalonian carol
Tune: EL CANT DELS OCELLS: Traditional Catalonian melody; harmonization AT, 1995

77. What is this lovely fragrance?
(Quelle est cette odeur agréable?)

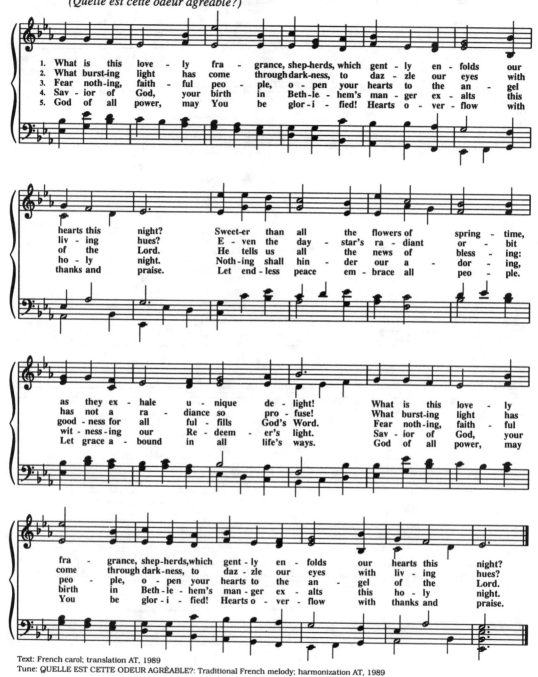

1. What is this love - ly fra - grance, shep-herds, which gent - ly en - folds our
2. What burst-ing light has come through dark-ness, to daz - zle our eyes with
3. Fear noth-ing, faith - ful peo - ple, o - pen your hearts to the an - gel
4. Sav - ior of God, your birth in Beth-le - hem's man - ger ex - alts this
5. God of all power, may You be glor - i - fied! Hearts o - ver - flow with

hearts this night? Sweet-er than all the flowers of spring - time,
liv - ing hues? E - ven the day - star's ra - diant or - bit
of the Lord. He tells us all the news of bless - ing:
ho - ly night. Noth-ing shall hin - der our a - dor - ing,
thanks and praise. Let end - less peace em - brace all peo - ple.

as they ex - hale u - nique de - light! What is this love - ly
has not a ra - diance so pro - fuse! What burst-ing light has
good - ness for all ful - fills God's Word. Fear noth-ing, faith - ful
wit - ness-ing our Re - deem - er's light. Sav - ior of God, your
Let grace a - bound in all life's ways. God of all power, may

fra - grance, shep-herds,which gent - ly en - folds our hearts this night?
come through dark-ness, to daz - zle our eyes with liv - ing hues?
peo - ple, o - pen your hearts to the an - gel of the Lord.
birth in Beth-le - hem's man - ger ex - alts this ho - ly night.
You be glor - i - fied! Hearts o - ver - flow with thanks and praise.

Text: French carol; translation AT, 1989
Tune: QUELLE EST CETTE ODEUR AGRÉABLE?: Traditional French melody; harmonization AT, 1989

78. What star is this with beams so bright

1. What star is this, with beams so bright, more
2. 'Tis now ful - filled what God de - creed: "From
3. While out - ward signs the star dis - plays, an
4. O while the star of heav'n - ly grace in -

love - ly than _____ the noon - day light? 'Tis
Ja - cob shall _____ a star pro - ceed;" and
in - ward light _____ the Lord con - veys, and
vites us, Lord, _____ to seek thy face, may

sent to an - nounce a new - born King, glad
lo! the east - ern sa - ges stand, to
urg - es them, with force be - nign, to
we no more that grace re - pel, or

tid - dings of our God to bring.
read in heav'n the Lord's com - mand.
seek the Giv - er of the sign.
quench that light which shines so well.

Text: Charles Coffin, 1736; translation *Hymns Ancient and Modern*, 1861, after John Chandler, 1837, alt.
Tune: PUER NOBIS NASCITUR: Melody from Trier MS., 15th C.; adapted Michael Praetorius, ca. 1600; harmonization *Cowley Carol Book*, 1902

79. What sweeter music can we bring

1. What sweet-er mu-sic can we bring than a ___ ca-rol, for to sing ___
2. Dark and dull night, fly hence a - way, and give the hon-our to this day, ___
3. The dar - ling of the world is come, and fit it is we find a room ___
4. which we will give him, and be - queath this hol-ly and this i - vy wreath,

___ the birth of this our heaven-ly King? ___ A - wake the ___ voice! A - wake the
___ that sees De - cem-ber turned to May, ___ if we may ___ ask the rea - son,
___ to wel - come him. The no - bler part ___ of all the ___ house here is the
___ to do him hon - our who's our King, ___ and Lord of ___ all this rev - el -

Refrain

string:
say:
heart:
ling:

We see him come ___ and know him ours, who with his sun -

shine and his showers, ___ turns all the pa - tient ground to flowers.

Text: Robert Herrick, 1647
Tune: HERRICK: Jack C. Goode, 1978

80. Whence comes this rush of wings afar

(Carol of the birds)

1. Whence comes this rush of wings a - far, fol - low - ing straight the No - el star? Birds of the woods in won - drous flight, Beth - le - hem seek this ho - ly night.

2. "Tell us, ye birds, why come ye here, in - to this sta - ble, poor and drear?" "Hast' - ning we seek the new - born King, and all our sweet - est mu - sic bring."

3. An - gels and shep - herds, birds of the sky, come where the Son of God doth lie; Christ on earth with man doth dwell, join in the shout, "No - el, no - el!"

Text: Traditional
Tune: NÖEL DES AUSELS: Traditional Bas-Quercy Carol

81. While by my sheep I watched
(Echo carol)

1. While by my sheep I watched at night, glad ti-dings brought an
2. There shall be born, so he did say, in Beth-le-hem a
3. There shall the Child lie in a stall, this Child who shall re-
4. This gift of God we'll cher-ish well, that ev-ery joy our

an - gel bright: How great my joy! Great my joy!
Child to - day. How great my joy! Great my joy!
deem us all. How great our joy! Great our joy!
hearts shall fill. How great our joy! Great our joy!

Joy, joy, joy! Joy, joy, joy! Praise we the Lord in

heaven on high! Praise we the Lord in heaven on high!

Text: Traditional German carol, 17th C.
Tune: ECHO CAROL: German melody, 17th C., arranged Hugo Jüngst, ca. 1890

82. Willie, get your sticks and drum
(Patapan)

1. Will - ie, get your sticks and drum, Rob - in, get your
2. Through the a - ges that have come, they have played the
3. Man and God are more at one than ___ are the

fife and come; as a hap - py Christ - mas
fife and drum, prais - ing Christ, the Son of
fife and drum. Thanks to God who sent His

band, tu - ra - lu - ra - lu, pat - a - pat - a - pan, as a
man, tu - ra - lu - ra - lu, pat - a - pat - a - pan, prais - ing
Son, tu - ra - lu - ra - lu, pat - a - pat - a - pan, thanks to

hap - py Christ - mas band let your mu - sic ___ fill the land.
Christ the Son of man and a King of ___ kings most grand!
God, who sent His Son with a song that's ___ just be - - gun!

Text: Traditional Burgundian carol, 17th C.; translation AT, 1995
Tune: PATAPAN: Burgundian carol, 17th C.; harmonization AT, 1995

83. Winds through the olive trees

1. Winds through the ol - ive trees, soft - ly did blow
2. Then from the hap - py skies, an - gels bent low,

'round lit - tle Beth - le - hem, long, long a - go.
sing - ing their songs of joy long, long a - go.

Sheep on the hill - side lay, whit - er than snow,
For in a man - ger bed, cra - dled, we know,

shep - herds were watch - ing them, long, long a - go.
Christ came to Beth - le - hem long, long a - go.

Text: Anonymous
Tune: Traditional; harmonization AT, 1995

Harmonization Copyright © 1995 DARCEY PRESS
P O box 5018, Vernon Hills, IL 60061

Where do our carols come from?

We sing our joy at Christmastime! We may call any piece we sing in that season a Christmas Carol. Is it a happy description of the season's celebrations? Is it a devotional portrayal of the events of Christ Jesus' birth? Surely, then, it is a Christmas Carol! But historically speaking, such a definition is very imprecise. This book includes what are more accurately defined as Christmas carols, Christmas hymns, and Christmas songs. Looking at the pieces themselves will help us to understand the differences. Consider first what we know about true carols.

Ancient carols began sometime during the Middle Ages (c. 500-1500 A.D.). Erik Routley, a distinguished musician and scholar and an expert on the history of church music, said carols were the music of the ordinary people at a time in history when they could not sing about their faith in church. In fact, ordinary people did not sing in church at all in those days; they only listened. They didn't even speak in church, and were quite content to leave everything to the priests and monks. So the vocal music ordinary people knew in those days were the plainsong they heard in church, sung by priests (later by small choirs of boys and men), and a more cheerful type of song, which ordinary people sang outside the church. Even when they wanted to sing about their faith, the people did it outside the church. And the music they sang was not written down; they had to remember it from hearing it before. Fortunately, their memories were strong because they exercised them a great deal more than we do ours.

Church-going in those days was not just a Sunday event. During the Middle Ages the church had numerous holy days - holidays - which would come into people's lives on all sorts of other days during the week. Nowadays we have special services for a few days, like Christmas, or Good Friday. In the Middle Ages there were many more than we have now. A town would drop everything on a holy day and go to Mass, and hear about a particular saint, or a particular holy event being celebrated that day. This was where the people learned Scripture; they couldn't read, and they surely couldn't have afforded to own the Bibles which took monks years to copy out by hand. The people heard the Bible being read, in Latin, in the church.

During the Middle Ages little **holy plays** began to be presented. These would take a passage of Scripture - a holy event - and act it out on the church steps. Later, such plays were taken to the people on carts (sometimes double decker carts, with the lower part a curtained dressing room). The plays would be performed in village streets on these movable stages, and the ordinary people could watch and have their memories refreshed about the event being portrayed.

The first Christmas manger scene we know of was created by St. Francis of Assisi in 1223, sharing with ordinary people a pictorial representation of the Nativity. In a cave near Grecchio, Italy, St. Francis brought animals, people, and a manger, to portray Christmas night and the holy birth. With special permission from the Pope, he conducted a Midnight Mass there. Carol-like songs were sung by the friars to accompany the tableau. *(Int'l Book of Carols, p. 5)*

The ancient carols existed for centuries without being written down, and their origins are impossible to confirm. **It is usually said that an ancient carol is a dance.** It is essentially a dance, but not like our dances today. Routley describes it like this:

> If you're dancing down the street there will be somebody singing as well as somebody playing, and there's only one person singing the story because only one person knows the words. All you know is the chorus [refrain]. So your dance consists of two parts - part when you're moving down the street and part when you're marking time, standing 'round in a circle. The part where you're marking time, standing 'round in a circle and listening to the singer, whom you can hear because you're near him, is called the <u>stanza</u> - the same word as "stand" - while the rest of it, the music, clapping, ringing of bells while you're running down the street to the next stanza - the next station - is called the burden [refrain].

> (Routley, *Christian Hymns*, tape 1B)

Carols portrayed many things besides Christmas events and traditions. Nor were the stories always Biblical. *The Oxford Book of Carols* has a wonderful selection of unusual carols.

To sum it all up, carols tell a story, using straightforward imagery. Often they have the stanza / refrain structure. Usually they have simple dancelike music. They often use language that fits everyday life. They may contain a dialogue between individual characters in the carol story. In this book, "Joseph *lieber*, Joseph mine" (48) shows the stanza / refrain pattern and has a dialogue. You can imagine the people standing in a circle with the singer, dancing in place as they listen to the stanza, and then dancing down the street as they all sing, "He comes to us this very day...."

Most of the written music we have from the Middle Ages is the music of the church. The plainsong melodies of the church had no measures, but were smooth and even. They were sung by the monks. Just as the monks were the ones copying out and writing down books in those days, so also they were the ones writing down music. Much of the written records we have of music in that time are what the monks wrote down - the even-note church plainsong form of the music.

There are three plainsong hymns included here (50, 57, 61). All three have a measured form, regularized so that congregations can sing them.

In the late Middle Ages an important invention was just coming into use. **By 1457, Johann Gutenberg made printing "practical" with his movable type printing press.** His press could print two pages of text at a time! Hand copying was no longer the only source of books. And as books became available, ordinary people began to learn to read.

In 1517, Martin Luther, a German Catholic priest, posted his 97 theses on the church door in Wittenberg. He protested certain practices of the Catholic Church of his day. Soon after that, he broke away from the Catholic Church, and the Protestant Reformation began.

One of Luther's grandest achievements was translating the Bible from Latin into German, the everyday language of the people (the vernacular). This translation, combined with the availability of movable type printing, made it increasingly possible for ordinary people to have a Bible, and in a form that they could read for themselves.

Luther's church services were in German, instead of the Latin of the Catholic Mass. And Luther, an enthusiastic musician, introduced hymns into the Lutheran Church services, music for ordinary people to sing in church. He would even take melodies of the popular music of the day and adapt them to fit the hymns. "Why should the devil get all the good tunes?" he asked.

Hymns, set to hymn tunes, have a more formal structure than carols. Rather than being story-like, a hymn typically stays close to Scripture and includes statements of Christian belief. Hymn tunes are usually not dance-like.

Everyone probably knows Luther's most famous hymn and tune, *"Ein' feste Burg ist unser Gott"* - "A mighty fortress is our God." He also wrote the carol, *"Vom Himmel hoch da komm' ich her"* - "From heaven high to earth I come" (36), for a Christmas Eve's entertainment in his home. It is based on an older folk song, *"Aus fremden Landen komm' ich her."* It has 15 stanzas.   A man dressed as an angel was to sing the first 7 stanzas, and the children greeted the angel by singing the remaining 8 stanzas.

By the 1800s, in England, the words of traditional carols were printed (without music) on sheets called "broadsides." Groups of English carolers called "Waits" traveled from house to house of the well-to-do, sang carols, and then were thanked with hot punch (wassail) and money. "The first nowell" (2) and several other carols in this collection come from that background. In "God rest you merry, gentlemen" (9), note the placement of the comma in the first line. The writer is saying "God preserve your happiness;" "merry" is not an adjective modifying "gentlemen." And it is good to remember that references to "men" include "women" as well, when the term is used in this general way.

There are many loved Christmas hymns from English sources. "Hark, the herald angels sing" (5), by Charles Wesley, and "Joy to the world" (18) by Isaac Watts, are two of everyone's favorites.

There are two "macaronic" carols in the book (carols which combine Latin with the vernacular). "The snow lay on the ground" (72) combines Latin with English, and comes from traditional English sources. *In dulci jubilo* is a macaronic carol coming from the German. John Mason Neale's English version of *"In dulci jubilo"* is called a paraphrase because it does not stay close to the original it translates. Neale's first line is, "Good Christian men, rejoice." This reference really refers to "men" generically, and therefore includes women. The text has been altered here. (The original first two lines, *"In dulci jubilo, nun singet und seid froh,"* translate to "In sweet rejoicing, now sing and be happy," and do not even refer to "men.")

Translations have given English versions of traditional carols from many foreign languages. See the Czech carol, "Rock-a-bye, my dear little boy" (66), and the Polish carol, "Infant holy, infant lowly" (45), for example. One of my new favorites is "'Twas in the moon of wintertime" (75), which is translated from the language of the Huron Indians of Canada, and uses their imagery .

In more recent times the simple story-like texts and the stanza / refrain style of the ancient carols continue to be used. See "We Three Kings" (16), which is written by an American. "That boy-child of Mary" (70), from Africa, uses the Christmas story to teach Christian beliefs to the people there.

We are indebted to many people for our carols! It's important to realize first that we're indebted to the people who remembered the carols before they were written down. We obviously are indebted to the original author / composer, whoever first thought up the words and, if a different person, whoever first thought up the music. Possibly we're indebted to a third person, who harmonized the melody when it was first written down. If the carols were not originally in English, we are indebted to the translator, who took the original words and translated them into a (rhyming) text to fit the carol tune. If a carol is relatively new, it is undoubtedly under copyright protection, so we are indebted to the copyright holder for giving permission to print the work. Then, of course, we are indebted to someone who finally takes all the elements - music with harmonization and translated words - and publishes them for us to sing and enjoy.

The credits here are listed at the bottom left of each piece. Anything which is credited "Traditional" comes from the memories of the people, and the name (or names) of the original source is lost. The dates on each item indicate as closely as possible the date of the first written-down appearance of the words or music. The first line of the credits gives the source of the words. This will include the origin, a translator if there has been one, and an indication if there have been any alterations ("alt.") to the text. The second line gives the source of the melody first, and then the harmonization if that has a different source. Copyright permissions are acknowledged where they were required.

There are wonderful stories behind many of the individual carols, and there are many places where you can find and read these stories. *The International Book of Carols* is the source of most of this story of "Silent night" *("Stille Nacht")*:

On Christmas Eve, 1818, Joseph Mohr, the assistant pastor of the Saint Nicholas Church in Oberndorf, Austria, brought to Franz Gruber, the organist, a poem he had written, and asked Gruber to write music for it for guitar and solo voices. The poem came at a critical moment: mice had eaten the leather of the church organ bellows, and the organ repair man was not going to get to the church to fix the bellows until after Christmas. This meant that all the pieces planned for the Christmas Eve service would not have the organ accompaniment they needed.

So Gruber set Mohr's hymn to music, and accompanied the singing on the guitar for that Christmas Eve Service. After Christmas, when the organ repairman came, Gruber played the carol for him. The repairman liked it so much that he took a copy with him when he left. He showed it to the Strasser sisters, a troupe of Tyrolean singers. They included it in their repertoire, and it quickly became a favorite with their audiences. And yet, even as it gained tremendous popularity, "... the names of Mohr and Gruber were never mentioned as its creators. Franz Joseph Haydn's son, Michael, was given credit for the carol in some published copies, possibly because he may have made an arrangement of the music. In 1854, 47 years after its composition, a special government committee was set up to try to determine who the creators of 'Silent night' were. They unearthed the facts through Felix Gruber, the son of Franz, who submitted [a] ... statement by his father ... , along with a copy of the original carol." (*Int'l Book of Carols*, p. 328)

One thing about the words of stanza one: the English translation, "Silent night," involves an enjambment - a place where a sentence of the text carries over beyond the end of the musical phrase. The sense of stanza one is: "Silent night, holy night, All is calm, all is bright [a]round [the] Virgin Mother and Child!", with the next thought: "Holy infant, so tender and mild, sleep in heavenly peace."

Following on the next page is **a new carol**. Although the text is story-like, it comes from two separate poems, which originally did not even have the same meter (number of syllables per line). The editor saw that the ideas of the two poems fit together nicely. So the meters of the two were regularized, and the resulting text was married to a tune and harmonization which would set them simply and well. Copyright permission was given to share the results here. You are invited to include it in your repertoire, - a new carol to express your joy of the season.

Merry Christmas!

Quotes and background on Middle Ages from Tape 1B of the audio book, *Christian Hymns: An Introduction to their Story*, by Dr. Erik Routley. Prestige Publications, 1980. ISBN 0-911-009-11-6.

See also:
The International Book of Christmas Carols, by Ehret and Evans; Walton, 1980. ISBN 0-8289-0378-6.
The Oxford Book of Carols, ed. Dearmer, Vaughan Williams, Shaw; Oxford University Press, 1928, 1974. Hardbound: ISBN 0 19 313104 8; Paperbound: ISBN 0 19 313120 X.

84. A village, humble, still

A Song of Bethlehem, Christmas Day

1. A vil - lage, hum - ble, still, _____ the guid - ing star a - bove; _____ a
2. The shep - herds brought their faith, _____ the wise - men of - fered gold _____ and

shep - herd watch - ing on a hill; the moth - er heart of love; _____ the
cost - ly frank - in - cense and myrrh; each brought his gift of old. _____ What

child of truth and grace, _____ a world to pac - i - fy; _____ an
shall we give to - day? _____ Wealth of the things of earth? _____ Or

an - gel song of _ joy - ous _ praise, and God to _ glor - i - fy.
hearts at - tuned to _ an - gel _ songs – and give our own new birth!

Text: Gertrude E. Velguth, st. 1, alt., 1956; Kathleen O'Connor, st. 2, alt., 1955. Reprinted with permission from
The Christian Science Sentinel. Copyright © 1956, 1955, The Christian Science Publishing Society. All rights reserved.

Tune: AIRIKAR: Adrienne M. Tindall, 1981; Harmonization: Erik Routley, 1981.
Music © 1997 Hope Publishing Co., Carol Stream, Il 60188. All rights reserved. Used with permission.

Index of Carols

** One verse of the original foreign language included

DARCEY PRESS offers...

Christmas Carols
for Friends and Families
with "Where do our carols come from?"

Regular Book, 6½" x 8½" (small book), 84 carols and rounds
ISBN 1-889079-21-9   **Price: $6.95**

Regular Book with singalong CD, with pipe organ
accompaniments for 40 of the 84 carols and rounds
ISBN 1-889079-37-5 Book with CD   **Price: $19.95**

Accompanist's book, 8½" x 11" size, spiral bound to lay flat
on the music rack
ISBN 1-889079-22-7   **Price: $26.95**

Special Order Packets:

"Family" Packet: 6 small books, 1 accompanist's book (save $10.00)
ISBN 1-889079-24-3   **Price: $58.65**

"Friends" Packet: 12 small books, 1 accompanist's book (save $20.00)
ISBN 1-889079-25 1   **Price: $90.35**

DARCEY PRESS
Box 5018, Vernon Hills, IL 60061
www.darceypress.com